The Wright Brothers

Marissa Hernandez

Contributing Author

Allison Duarte, M.A.

Consultants

Tamieka Grizzle, Ed.D.
K–5 STEM Lab Instructor
Harmony Leland Elementary School

Russ Lee
Curator
Smithsonian

Publishing Credits

Rachelle Cracchiolo, M.S.Ed., *Publisher*
Conni Medina, M.A.Ed., *Managing Editor*
Diana Kenney, M.A.Ed., NBCT, *Content Director*
Véronique Bos, *Creative Director*
June Kikuchi, *Content Director*
Robin Erickson, *Art Director*
Seth Rogers, *Editor*
Mindy Duits, *Senior Graphic Designer*
Smithsonian Science Education Center

Image Credits: front cover, p.1 (portrait) Apic/Getty Images; back cover, pp.2–3, p.4, p.7, p.8, pp.10–11, p.11 (insert), p.14, p.15, p.18, p.20, p.22, p.23, p.32 © Smithsonian; p.5 (top) csfotoimages/iStock; p.5 (bottom), p.9 Dorling Kindersle/Getty Images; p.9 (bottom) Library of Congress [LC-USZ62-127779]; p.16 Library of Congress [LC-DIG-ppprs-00650]; p.17 Granger Academic; p.19 Jim Sugar/Corbis/Getty Images; p.21 Ed Vebell/Getty Images; p.25 Leemage/Getty Images; p.27 (top) U.S. Air Force; p.31 Peter Spiro/iStock; all other images from iStock and/or Shutterstock.

Library of Congress Cataloging-in-Publication Data

Names: Hernandez, Marissa, author.
Title: The Wright brothers / Marissa Hernandez.
Description: Huntington Beach, CA : Teacher Created Materials, [2019] |
  Includes index. | Audience: K to Grade 3.
Identifiers: LCCN 2017056317 (print) | LCCN 2018002288 (ebook) | ISBN
  9781493869244 (e-book) | ISBN 9781493866847 (pbk.)
Subjects: LCSH: Wright, Orville, 1871-1948--Juvenile literature. | Wright,
  Wilbur, 1867-1912--Juvenile literature. | Aeronautics--United
  States--History--20th century--Juvenile literature. | Inventors--United
  States--History--20th century--Juvenile literature. | CYAC:
  Aeronautics--United States. | Inventors--United States.
Classification: LCC TL540.W7 (ebook) | LCC TL540.W7 H475 2019 (print) | DDC
  629.130092/273 [B] --dc23
LC record available at https://lccn.loc.gov/2017056317

Teacher Created Materials

5301 Oceanus Drive
Huntington Beach, CA 92649-1030
www.tcmpub.com

ISBN 978-1-4938-6684-7
© 2019 Teacher Created Materials, Inc.
Printed in China
51497

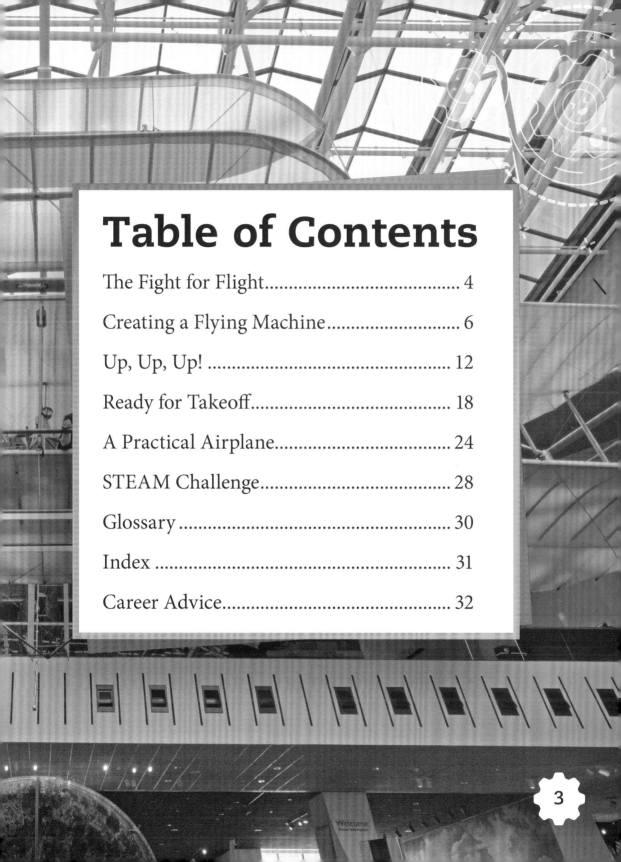

Table of Contents

The Fight for Flight

Orville and Wilbur Wright were brothers. From an early age, they liked to experiment. They wanted to build a flying **machine**. Both had worked on printing presses and motors. They also owned a bicycle shop. With the same tools they used to fix the bikes in their shop, the brothers built a **glider**. It used wind to rise off the ground, just like a kite!

The Wright brothers spent years improving the design of the glider. Their goal was to build a machine that would lift a person into the sky. For years, many people dreamed of manned flight. But nobody had ever done it. The Wright brothers were sure that they could be the ones to finally make the dream a reality.

There would be many problems along the way. Countless hours would be spent studying and testing their plans. It would take a lot of hard work if they wanted to become the fathers of flight.

Orville Wright (right) works at the bicycle shop with his friend Edwin H. Sines (left).

Wilbur and
Orville Wright

Creating a Flying Machine

The Wright brothers were inventors. They took what they knew and applied it to new ideas. They knew how bicycles worked. This helped them plan the design of their glider.

Just like Riding a Bike

Riding a bike is similar to flying an airplane. Both need balance and control. Both machines need a strong frame built out of light materials. The materials need to be wind resistant and have an aerodynamic shape. This helps with stability.

For years, the Wright brothers studied how things fly. They researched birds and wings. They looked at the shapes, sizes, and angles that allow birds to fly. One thing they noticed was how birds warped, or twisted, their wings to help them turn in the air. This led them to an idea for how they could turn their flying machine.

Eagles use wing warping to turn in the air.

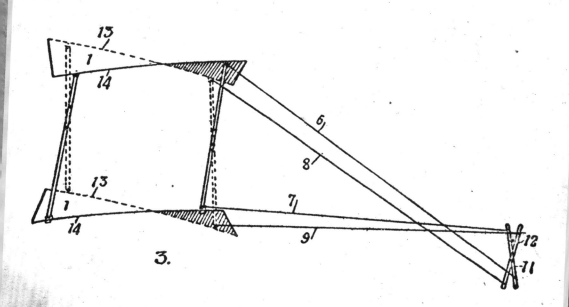

3.

ENGINEERING

Wing Warping

Wing warping is one way to control an airplane. It is a system of cables that twist the edge of the wings in opposite directions. This allows a plane to turn by leaning more to the right or left. The Wright brothers found that this was an easy way to maneuver planes. Wing warping is similar to flying a paper airplane. If the tips of the wing are curled back, it glides and turns.

Building the Glider

Before the Wright brothers built a glider, they tested wing warping on a kite. This was not an ordinary kite. The Wright Kite was shaped like a box and was 2 meters (6 feet) long. It also had large wings on each side that could twist and turn. The brothers' goal was to see whether changing the shape and angle of the wings would help steer a plane. They were right! The Wright Kite was balanced and controlled. Orville and Wilbur were ready to start building a glider.

The first glider was a larger version of the Wright Kite. The brothers mainly focused on the shape and size of the wings. Through their research, they knew that the wings had to be slightly curved in the front and straighter in the back. They also found that the wings had to be very large for balance.

1900 Wright Glider

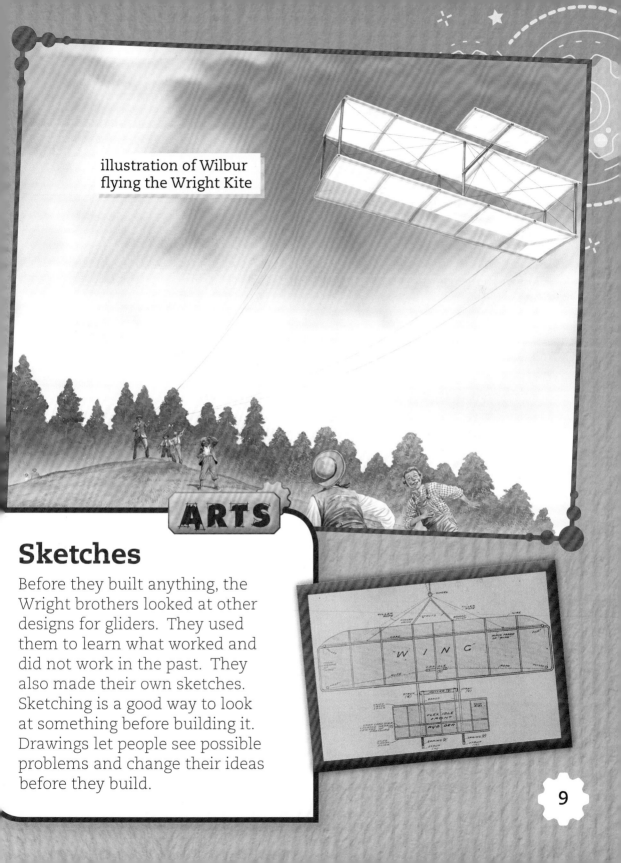

illustration of Wilbur flying the Wright Kite

ARTS

Sketches

Before they built anything, the Wright brothers looked at other designs for gliders. They used them to learn what worked and did not work in the past. They also made their own sketches. Sketching is a good way to look at something before building it. Drawings let people see possible problems and change their ideas before they build.

The glider had to be sturdy. The brothers used pinewood to build the wings and wing struts. Wing struts are poles that hold the top and bottom wings together. Special fabric was wrapped around the wooden wings. This would help keep the wings together if the glider made a hard landing.

The brothers were ready to test their first glider. They launched the machine in Kitty Hawk, North Carolina. The area was known for having wide-open spaces and strong winds. The Wrights first tried flying the glider as a kite. This let them test how high and steady the glider could get. The brothers successfully flew the glider as a kite several times. Then, a gust of wind made it crash. They had more work to do. They went back home to start over.

This photo shows the 1900 Glider after it crashed.

Tom Tate was a young boy who helped the Wright brothers fly the first glider. Because he was small, he would lie in the middle of the glider while the brothers controlled the glider from the ground.

Up, Up, Up!

The Wright brothers came home with more ideas. They knew the design and structure of the glider were right. The controls of the glider also worked. But the brothers wanted the next glider to have more **lift** to keep it in the air. This meant their design needed to change.

The Next Glider

They looked at the wings again. They believed bigger wings would give the glider more lift. To get the right size, they calculated lift. They also calculated how much **drag** would hold the plane back. And they changed the type of fabric wrapped around the wings.

Even though they made many changes, this glider did not work either. It still did not have enough lift. The glider was also hard to control. The brothers were very disappointed. Their hard work had not yet paid off.

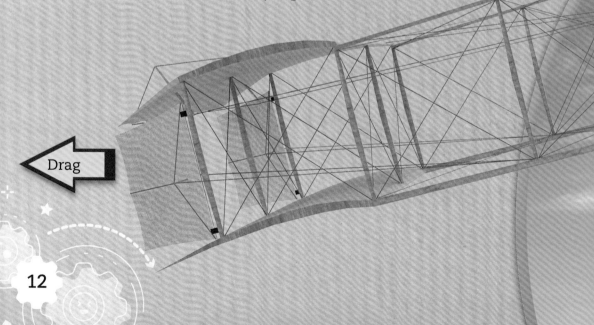

Drag

The Four Forces

There are four forces that affect how things fly. *Weight* is the force of gravity, which pulls a plane down. *Lift* moves a plane upward. It is created by the wings of a plane. *Thrust* moves a plane forward in motion with force created by an engine. *Drag* pulls a plane back, in the opposite direction of motion. The four forces need to balance out one another for a plane to successfully fly.

Lift

Thrust

Weight

The 1902 Glider

The Wright brothers got back to work. The glider's lift and drag were big problems. This meant they had to experiment before building again.

They spent a lot of time looking at how the four forces—weight, lift, thrust, and drag—acted on a glider. The first big change was a new control system. While the plane was flying, it would be able to tilt its nose up and down, changing the pitch. It could tilt its wings up and down, known as roll. The tail could also turn the plane left or right, which is known as yaw. For the first time, a flying machine could be fully controlled.

The brothers were ready for another test. They wanted to make sure the structure and control were right. They went back to Kitty Hawk. Just like they did before, the brothers first flew this glider like a kite. The results were good. The glider had enough lift, and the flight controls worked.

In 1902, the Wright brothers run their glider through its third test.

14

wind tunnel

TECHNOLOGY

New Inventions

The Wright brothers invented two devices to test their glider. The first looked like a regular bicycle with an extra wheel on the handlebars. It measured air pressure and wing angles. The second was a wind tunnel (shown above), which was a wooden box with a fan and an engine inside. The engine made wind. This let them test the control of a glider without the risk of it crashing.

It was time for the Wright brothers to test the glider themselves. There was no seat. They lay in the middle of the wings. It worked. They did it! Now, it was time to change their glider into a flyer by giving it thrust.

The 1903 Flyer

The brothers still had a lot of work to do. They needed to add an engine and propellers. This would give the flyer thrust. The engine was heavy. They would need to change the size of the wings of the flyer to add lift. The flyer had to be stronger to hold the extra weight of the engine.

The brothers built their own engine. They also invented a propeller and transmission system to give it thrust. The flight controls from the glider were used on the flyer. The Wrights built it and headed back to Kitty Hawk. This time, they were going to test their first powered airplane.

motor of the 1903 Flyer

painting of the 1903
Flyer at Kitty Hawk

MATHEMATICS

Wing Sizes

The Wright brothers changed the size of the
wings many times. They had to figure out how
big the wings needed to be. To do this, they
used math. They divided the wingspan by the
wing area. This gave them the information that
helped them solve the lift and drag problem.

Ready for Takeoff

The Wright brothers worked on their flyer for three months. They waited for good weather. Everything had to be perfect for takeoff.

Launching Rail

Since the flyer was larger than the gliders, the brothers had to change the way it took off. They could not hold the ends of the glider to launch it into the air. The flyer was too heavy and complex to do this. So they built another device. It was a **launching rail**. It was made of four long metal pieces that created a track. The brothers wanted the flyer to move down the track to gain speed and then take off.

They were nervous, but the brothers were ready. After many years of working on a flying machine, they knew it was time.

The Wright Flyer is ready for flight in 1903.

The flyer was heavier than the brothers thought it would be. It weighed 274 kilograms (605 pounds)!

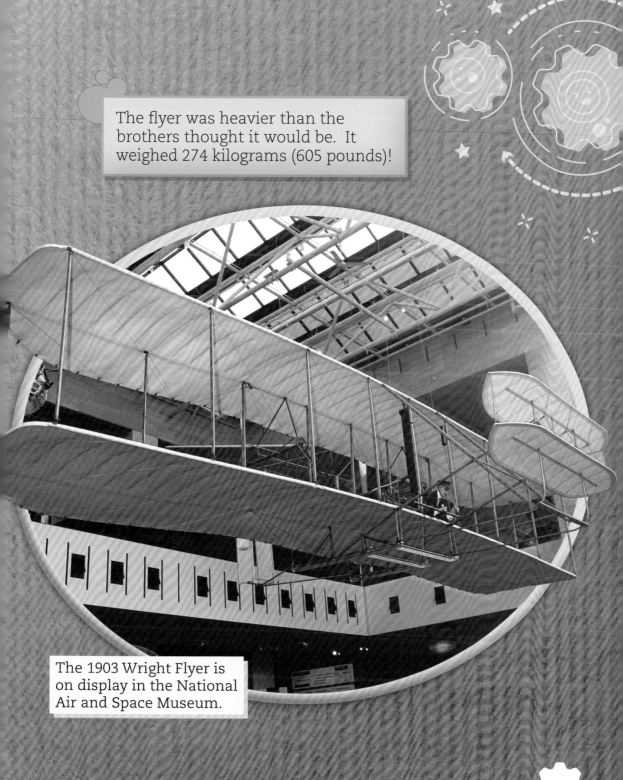

The 1903 Wright Flyer is on display in the National Air and Space Museum.

The First Human Flight

The Wright brothers put their flyer to the test. On a cold December day, Wilbur climbed on board and headed to the launching rail. The flyer went down the tracks and lifted up, but it stalled and crashed into the sand. The brothers were still hopeful. They fixed the flyer and tried again three days later.

This time, Orville was the pilot. It went down the launching rail and stayed up for 12 seconds. Although this was a short time, it proved that the flyer worked! The Wright brothers had made history. It was the first manned, controlled flight on a fully powered airplane.

The brothers made three more flights that day. Each time, the flyer traveled farther and longer. The final trip lasted 59 seconds and traveled 260 m (853 ft.) before landing. The brothers made humans fly!

Orville was the first to stay in the air.

The Wright brothers flipped a coin to see who would get to ride the flyer first. Wilbur won.

illustration of the first flight at Kitty Hawk

But the journey was not over. The Wright brothers were not finished with aviation. They continued to work on more flyers. Their next goal was to build an even better plane that would stay in the air for a longer period of time.

The 1904 Flyer

The brothers began to work on a new flyer. They wanted it to stay in the air longer. The first flyer had the right controls, but it was not stable. The next one had to be more reliable.

The brothers added more weight to the front of the flyer. This improved balance. Then, they moved the elevator. This controlled the pitch and lift of the wings. With these changes, the 1904 Flyer had an improved design. It was the first plane that flew in a complete circle.

The 1904 Wright Flyer made a total of 105 flights.

Wilbur (left) and Orville (right) sit outside their home in 1909.

A Practical Airplane

After the circular flight, the brothers knew their flying machine was on the right track. But there were more changes to be made. The Wrights built one more flyer in 1905. They doubled the size of the elevator. The flyer had much more control. They could fly this plane longer than any of the others. Now, they were ready to show their flyer to the world.

People did not believe them at first. They thought the brothers were lying about their flights. The Wrights went to many places around the world to show their flyers in action. Everyone was amazed. Wilbur and Orville Wright became known as the forefathers of manned flight.

After that, the brothers started the Wright Company. They built and sold many airplanes. They even worked with the U.S. military on planes.

The 1905 Flyer is on display in Dayton, Ohio. This is where the Wright brothers were from. It is where they built most of their flying machines.

Dayton, Ohio

In 1908, Wilbur flies a plane in France.

Flying Today

Wilbur and Orville Wright are proof that testing and improving an idea works. They wanted to build a machine that would help people fly. And they did it! But that wasn't the end of their journey. They kept working to make their designs better.

The brothers changed the world. It didn't take long for airplanes to become a common way to travel. Less than 20 years after the first test flight, people flew across the ocean! Many of the same concepts from the Wright Flyer are used to build airplanes today. Many of the controls that the Wright brothers invented are still used. The world owes a lot to the two bike shop owners who had dreams of flying.

Orville (left) and Wilbur (right) only flew together once. It was in 1910. They both rode on a flyer for a total of six minutes.

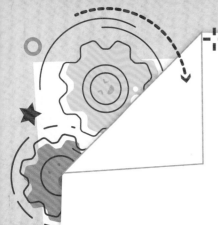

STEAM CHALLENGE

Define the Problem

Wilbur and Orville Wright changed their design many times before the first manned flight in 1903. They experimented with many parts of their gliders and flyers. Your challenge is to put one of their ideas to the test. Can you design a glider to transport cargo?

Constraints: You may only use paper and tape to build your glider.

Criteria: The glider must transport cargo (10 paperclips) a distance of 4 meters.

Research and Brainstorm

How did Wilbur and Orville Wright experiment with adding weight to their gliders and flyers? What did they find? Where could a glider hold extra weight?

Design and Build

Plan the design of your glider. You may find and use folding instructions online and adjust the design or create your own from scratch. Where will you add the paperclips to the glider? How will you secure the paperclips? Build the glider and add the cargo.

Test and Improve

Test the glider twice, and write down the longest distance the glider flies. How can you improve the glider? Will you move the cargo? Modify your design, and try again.

Reflect and Share

Could you use a different material to make the gliders? What other parts of the paper gliders could be changed? Could you add more cargo to your glider?

Glossary

aerodynamic—something that has been designed for motion in the air

aviation—having to do with the operation of aircraft

drag—the force that acts against the movement of an object

elevator—part of a plane that controls the plane's angle up or down

flyer—a flying machine that uses an engine; an airplane

glider—an aircraft that does not use an engine

launching rail—a set of tracks that help a plane with takeoff

lift—a force that acts to hold a plane up in the air

machine—a device with moving parts that uses power to do work

pitch—slant or angle of an object up and down

roll—tilt or angle of an object from side to side

stability—the quality or state of being steady and not easily changing

transmission—the part of an engine that turns the power of the engine into the spinning of wheels

yaw—turning an object from right to left

Index

CAREER ADVICE
from Smithsonian

Do you want to design airplanes?
Here are some tips to get you started.

"Airplane designers use math and science skills, so study hard in those classes. The next time you're on an airplane, notice how it pitches, yaws, and rolls. These play an important role in how a plane flies. Try putting together model airplanes—that's how I learned about planes as a kid!" —**Russ Lee, Chair, Aeronautics Department**

"We can learn so much from the Wright brothers, especially the fact that they never gave up. They designed, built, and tested their gliders and planes. Then, they made improvements. Creativity and problem solving are an important part of STEAM. If you want to design planes or trains or buildings or highways, you must have that same tenacity." —**Mike Hulslander, "How Things Fly" Gallery Manager**